CW00385968

THE
GREAT WESTERN
IN NORTH WALES

• A PAST and PRESENT COMPANION •

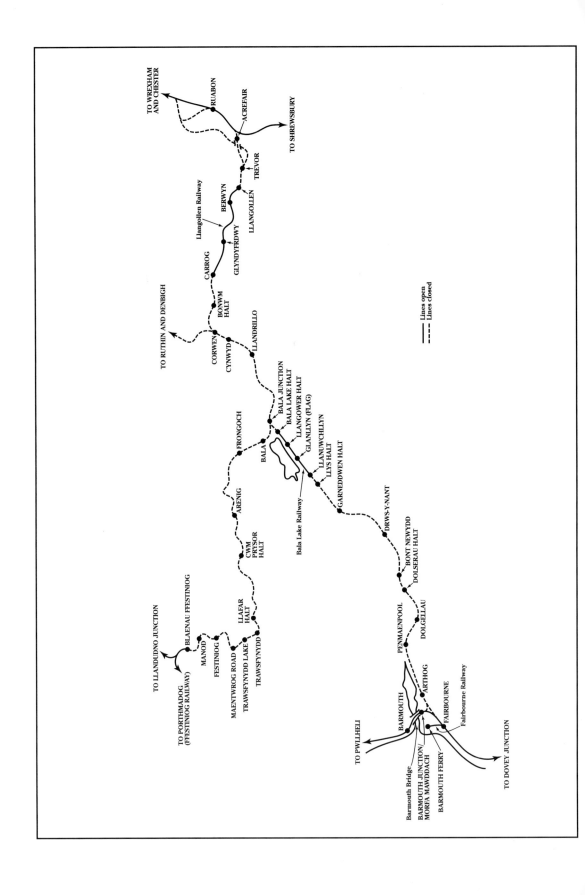

THE
GREAT WESTERN
IN NORTH WALES

·A PAST AND PRESENT COMPANION·

Including the Llangollen, Bala Lake and Fairbourne railways

John Hillmer and Paul Shannon

·RAILWAY HERITAGE·

from

The NOSTALGIA Collection

© John Hillmer and Paul Shannon 2007

All rights reserved. No part of this publication may be reproduced, stored in a retrieval system or transmitted, in any form or by any means, electronic, mechanical, photocopying, recording or otherwise, without prior permission in writing from Past & Present Publishing Ltd.

First published in 2007

British Library Cataloguing in Publication Data

A catalogue record for this book is available from the British Library.

ISBN 978 1 85895 255 0

Past & Present Publishing Ltd
The Trundle
Ringstead Road
Great Addington
Kettering
Northants NN14 4BW

Tel/Fax: 01536 330588
email: sales@nostalgiacollection.com
Website: www.nostalgiacollection.com

Printed and bound in Great Britain

Past and Present

A Past & Present book
from
The NOSTALGIA *Collection*

CARROG: 4300 Class 2-6-0 No 7300 arrives at Carrog with a westbound train on 13 May 1961. The 89B shedplate on the smokebox door denotes Croes Newydd, the main source of traction for the Ruabon-Barmouth line. The sheds at Bala, Penmaenpool and Trawsfynydd were all sub-sheds of Croes Newydd, with no specific allocation of their own.

On 1 May 2006 2800 Class 2-8-0 No 3802 runs round its train before returning to Llangollen with the 1400 departure. The 6C shedplate also denotes Croes Newydd, changed from 89B after the transfer of former GWR lines in North Wales from the Western Region to the London Midland Region in 1963. Like the signal box, the shelter on the down platform is a remarkably authentic copy of the original. *Bryan Wilson, courtesy of The Transport Treasury/PDS*

CONTENTS

LLANUWCHLLYN: 2MT 2-6-0 No 46446, which was much photographed on the line, stands in front of the signal box awaiting the arrival of a down train before departing to Bala Junction on 19 December 1964.

In the 'present' picture it can be seen that the trackbed now carries the narrow-gauge Bala Lake Railway. The locomotive, *Alice*, was built by Hunslet in 1902, and worked at Dinorwic Quarries until around 1960, sister engine to *Holy War*; note that she has no cab protection for the crew. She was used for spares, then the remains were gathered together in 1977 and restoration commenced in 1987. After spending time at the Ffestiniog Railway and the Leighton Buzzard Railway, *Alice* returned to her present home in 2003. In the distance beyond the station can be seen the water tank. *Gavin Morrison/JCH*

INTRODUCTION

Few former railway routes in the British Isles rival those from Ruabon to Barmouth and from Bala Junction to Blaenau Ffestiniog for their natural beauty and for their wealth of historical interest, much of it brought to life again today by the efforts of preservation volunteers.

Historically the Ruabon to Barmouth line gave the Great Western Railway its highly prized access to the Welsh coast and Barmouth for holiday traffic. The route also passed through some of the most delightful landscapes in Wales, including the Vale of Llangollen, Bala Lake and the picturesque Mawddach Estuary, dominated by Cader Idris on its southern side.

Apart from the larger towns of Llangollen, Corwen, Dolgellau and Barmouth, the line to the coast took in some very lonely places such as Garneddwen, Drws-y-Nant and Bont Newydd. Even more isolated were the localities served by tiny halts on the branch line from Bala Junction to Blaenau Ffestiniog, where the business generated by farm-workers and walkers can never have been significant.

However, if passengers were scarce, many rural stations were busy with goods traffic until the rapid growth of road transport after the Second World War. Livestock and agricultural supplies kept station goods yards alive, and there was industry too, such as the slate mines at Blaenau Ffestiniog and quarries at Arenig. Even in its last months the Bala to Blaenau Ffestiniog line carried large tonnages of cement for the building of Trawsfynydd nuclear power station.

Four decades after the closure of most of the lines and stations pictured in this book, links with the past are very obvious at some locations but difficult or impossible to find at others. In some of the scenes on the restored Llangollen Railway it is not immediately clear which picture belongs to the 'past' and which to the 'present'; we have included several intermediate views of dereliction to show how much work needed to be done. A different example of preservation is found at Bala Lake, where a delightful narrow-gauge railway follows the course of the former standard-gauge line. We have also taken the liberty of including the narrow-gauge Fairbourne Railway, which was very much associated with the Cambrian Coast line and gave an alternative access to Barmouth via the ferry from Penrhyn Point.

As for the abandoned stretches, no traces remain of many of the stations, which have either been commercially redeveloped or returned to nature. However, a notable exception is Bala Junction, where the grass-covered and sheep-grazed platforms provide an uncanny link with the past. A few station buildings survive in non-railway use, such as Corwen, Trawsfynydd and Maentwrog Road. One of the most delightful former railway locations is Penmaenpool, once the site of a small locomotive shed and still strongly retaining its railway atmosphere, even though the clatter of trains is a distant memory.

It has been a great privilege and pleasure for us to put this book together and we hope that the readers will share with us the same delights in absorbing it.

Paul Shannon, Chester
John Hillmer, Wilmslow

BIBLIOGRAPHY

ABC British Railways Locomotives, combined volumes, various years (Ian Allan)
Butt, R. V. J. *Directory of Railway Stations* (Patrick Stephens Ltd)
Locomotive Stock Books, 1966 and 1969 (Railway Correspondence & Travel Society)
Rear, W. G. and Jones, N. *Scenes from the Past 9: The Llangollen line, Ruabon to Barmouth* (Foxline)
Smith, Paul *Steam Motive Power Depots* Volume 2 (Platform 5)
Southern, D. *Scenes from the Past 25: Bala Junction to Blaenau Ffestiniog* (Foxline)
Wignall, C. J. *Complete British Railways Maps and Gazetteer 1830-1981* (OPC)

ACKNOWLEDGEMENTS

The authors are grateful to the many photographers who provided material for use in this book, to Dave Southern for supplying a wealth of detailed information as well as for his generosity in loaning historic photographs, to Ralph Rawlinson and Bryan Wilson for information about the lines, to Geraldine Hillmer for expertise with digital images, to Air Products Limited for access to its Acrefair works, and to the staff of the Llangollen Railway, Bala Lake Railway and Fairbourne Railway – especially Roger Hine and Colin Jepson – for their practical help and advice.

Ruabon to Llangollen

RUABON: Advertisements ranging from cocoa to insurance rank among the less obvious features of this fascinating snapshot from the late 19th century. Most of the station facilities at Ruabon were concentrated here on the up platform, although there were further buildings, including refreshment rooms, on the down platform. The station, goods yard and local signal boxes provided employment for more than 100 people at that time. The sign 'PASSENGERS ARE REQUESTED TO CROSS THE LINE BY THE BRIDGE' seems tamely worded by today's standards.

Ruabon became an unstaffed halt in 1974 but the up-side building has survived to the present day, albeit bereft of its awnings. Unit No 158849 draws to a halt forming the 1528 Chester to Birmingham New Street service on 30 September 2006. *Mrs Gwyneth Williams collection/PDS*

RUABON: This was the view from the up platform, facing south, in early BR days. Two members of the station staff stop for a moment to watch the shunting taking place in the down sidings. The goods depot on the up side looks busy and the nameboard on the down platform proudly announces: 'RUABON JUNCTION FOR LLANGOLLEN BALA BARMOUTH & PWLLHELI'. Ruabon Middle signal box is visible just beyond the goods shed.

The differing platform lengths and the lattice footbridge, now without its roof, confirm that the 'present' photograph is taken from the same vantage point. Units 158827 and 158818 arrive forming the 0720 Cardiff Central to Holyhead service on 30 September 2006. The sidings at Ruabon were removed in the early 1970s, while the structure of Ruabon Middle box lasted until 1987, some time after it ceased to be regularly manned. *Lens of Sutton Collection/PDS*

LLANGOLLEN LINE JUNCTION: The Llangollen branch diverged from the Shrewsbury to Chester line just over half a mile south of Ruabon station. Originally the Llangollen branch was single track but it was doubled in 1898. Stanier Class 5 No 45184 rattles over the junction on the main line with a Chester-bound train in the mid-1950s.

After the end of goods traffic to Llangollen in 1968 there was no further use for the branch and Llangollen Line Junction ceased to exist. The branch formation is now overgrown, as pictured on 30 September 2006. *Norman Kneale/PDS*

ACREFAIR was the first station out of Ruabon on the Llangollen line. Entering the station on 25 August 1962 is 4300 Class 2-6-0 No 5330 with a Ruabon to Barmouth service. Gas lamps are visible on both platforms and the small goods yard on the down side is evidently still in use.

The former station site now forms part of the Air Products compound, as pictured on 30 September 2006. The industrial buildings have changed except for the brick building with its roof ridge parallel to the railway alignment, which is seen in both photographs. Forty years of tree growth have obscured the hillside through which the railway once carved its path. *P. J. Garland collection/PDS*

ACREFAIR: The population of Acrefair grew rapidly in the late 19th century as the railway helped to fuel the growth of coal mines, brickworks and other industries. In this delightful Victorian scene a Ruabon-bound goods train passes over the bridge almost unnoticed by the children standing in the traffic-free main street.

No trace remains of the former railway bridge and the houses on the north side of the street have been demolished; however, those on the south side appear to have survived with only minor alterations. The 'present' scene is dated 1 May 2006. *John Ryan collection/PDS*

TREVOR: Local industries between Trevor and Acrefair were served by the Pontcysyllte mineral branch, which diverged from the main Llangollen line at Trevor. This was the view looking towards Trevor on 6 September 1952, with the brickworks on the right still active but the railway spur to Pontcysyllte, which used to run immediately to the left of the high stone wall, now removed.

A remnant of the mineral railway remained in use until the mid 1960s, but today the embankment is heavily overgrown, as pictured on 1 May 2006. It is just possible to make out the same shed on the left of the 'present' and 'past' pictures. *John Ryan collection/PDS*

TREVOR station, just under 2 miles west of Llangollen Line Junction, was once an important source of passenger and goods traffic. 4300 Class 2-6-0 No 7313 enters the station with a westbound train on 15 April 1958.

The road overbridge is just visible through the thicket of sycamore, ash and willow trees growing on the former trackbed and platforms on 3 June 2006. *H. B. Priestley, David Southern collection/PDS*

15

TREVOR: An unidentified Pannier tank awaits departure from the down sidings at Trevor with a typical pick-up goods train of the early BR era, comprising three vans, two mineral wagons and a brake-van. These sidings were the departure point for the Pontcysyllte branch, but also acted as the headshunt for Trevor goods yard, located behind the photographer. The gate on the far right belonged to the Roberts & McGinnis brickyard siding, another source of freight revenue at this busy location.

A pleasant public footpath now follows the former trackbed west of Trevor, as pictured on 3 June 2006. *Brian Taylor/PDS*

LLANGOLLEN: Approaching Llangollen station from the east in June 1963 is Ivatt Class 2 2-6-0 No 46507 with a rake of non-corridor stock. The Ivatt 2-6-0s became more common on the Llangollen line in later years, foreshadowing the transfer of the route from Western to London Midland Region control in September 1963.

Trees everywhere! Not only is the former trackbed obscured, but even the River Dee is partly masked by tree growth. Scarcely any recognisable features are shared by the 'past' scene and the 'present' photograph of 30 September 2006. *R. H. Robinson/ PDS*

The Llangollen Railway

Once the Ruabon to Barmouth line had been earmarked for closure in the 1963 Beeching Report, its decline was rapid. Through freight traffic west of Llangollen ceased in November 1964 and within a month severe flooding brought the sudden demise of the route between Llangollen and Bala Junction. Llangollen then became a temporary terminus for the passenger service from Ruabon until that ceased on 16 January 1965, freight services on that stretch lingering until March 1968.

BR was quick to lift the track after closure, but much of the railway formation remained intact, as did some of the platforms and station buildings. This provided an excellent opportunity for the then recently formed Flint & Deeside Railway Preservation Society to revive an interesting section of railway with good tourist potential. In 1975 the society took a lease on the first 3 miles of the route west of Llangollen, with the eventual aim of reaching Corwen.

Tracklaying in Llangollen station began in the summer of 1975, using redundant rails from Courtaulds. A further donation of track from Shell UK Oil Ltd enabled volunteers to begin the long and arduous task of extending towards Berwyn. A Fowler diesel shunter was the first of many locomotives that would be acquired for the railway over the next few years. Meanwhile the Flint & Deeside Railway Preservation Society was superseded by the Llangollen Railway Society in 1977.

The first passenger-carrying service since 1964 operated from Llangollen to the temporary end of the line at Ffordd Junction, about half a mile away, on 26 July 1981. Thereafter, thanks to donations of materials, money and time, the railway was extended to Berwyn in 1985, Deeside Halt in 1990, Glyndyfrdwy in 1992 and Carrog in 1996. Missing signal boxes and station buildings were either built from scratch or imported from other parts of the GWR network, gradually recreating an authentic atmosphere.

Today the Llangollen Railway operates trains every day in the summer season and during school holidays, as well as most weekends throughout the year. Special events range from the ever-popular Thomas the Tank Engine weeks to diesel and steam galas. Almost 200 volunteers share the task of keeping the railway going and the stock list includes seven operational steam locomotives, 11 diesel locomotives and a wide range of DMUs, carriages and freight vehicles. The eventual goal is still Corwen, where a new station is expected to be built on the east side of the town.

LLANGOLLEN: The classic view of Llangollen station from the road bridge over the River Dee is seen in 1960, with Pannier tank No 3630 setting out for Ruabon with a well-loaded mixed goods train. The short siding on the right was once used to load and unload horse-boxes; the main goods facilities in Llangollen were situated beyond the west end of the station, hidden behind the houses in this photograph.

The second photograph shows just how much work the volunteers of the Flint & Deeside Railway Preservation Society had let themselves in for. This was the scene shortly after closure in 1968, with tracklifting imminent.

On 3 June 2006 Class 20 diesel-electric No D8142 runs round its coaches at the same location after working the 1300 departure from Carrog. The period atmosphere recreated today is a testimony to the hard work of dozens of volunteers over the past 30 years – work that included relaying all the track as well as restoring the signal box and station buildings. *N. R. Knight/C. L. Caddy collection/PDS*

LLANGOLLEN: The eastern exit from Llangollen is pictured during a quiet moment on Saturday 25 August 1962. The starting signal at the end of the up platform is 'off', suggesting that the signal box is switched out. The one-time trailing crossover between the running lines has been removed, but the up siding remains in place. The whole scene is remarkably neat and tidy, belying the fact that passenger services would end less than three years later.

The relaying of track began in 1975, although it was not until 1981 that the first passenger-carrying train operated on the revived line. A facing crossover was provided roughly on the site of the former trailing crossover, and new signals were installed to control run-round movements. Beneath the bridge the track ends abruptly at a wall; any prospect of extending the railway eastwards is very remote. On 30 September 2006 'Manor' Class 4-6-0 No 7822 *Foxcote Manor* starts its run-round manoeuvre after arrival with the 1150 train from Carrog. *P. J. Garland collection/PDS*

LLANGOLLEN: This east-facing view from the down platform shows the tight location of the station above the River Dee, with the end of the footbridge overhanging the water. A pair of 4300 Class 2-6-0s, with No 6307 leading, heads a westbound rake of pre-nationalisation coaching stock.

The bunting in the 'present' view of 30 September 2006 is not for the Eisteddfod but rather to mark the first wedding ceremony to take place on the Llangollen Railway, with the couple set to enjoy a wedding breakfast on the move behind *Foxcote Manor* after tying the knot in the station offices. The service train pictured here is the 1350 departure from Carrog. *David Southern collection/PDS*

LLANGOLLEN station had unusually long platforms, with ramped access at the west end providing an easy means of entrance and exit for visitors to the Eisteddfod; however, the gates at the top of the ramps were locked shut in normal traffic conditions. Entering the up platform on 15 August 1953 are 4300 Class 2-6-0s Nos 4375 and 6344 with the 8.45 train from Pwllheli. More than 300 locomotives of this class were built between 1911 and 1932, but only two survive in preservation today – Nos 5322 and 7325.

A small group of admirers witnesses the tender-first arrival of *Foxcote Manor* with the 1400 train from Carrog on 1 May 2006. The ramps are now in regular use and the signalling allows westbound departures from either platform. *H. C. Casserley/PDS*

PENTREFELIN: A short spur just west of Llangollen gave access to a wharf on the Llangollen Canal and provided a rail outlet for Pentrefelin slate works. In later years Pentrefelin had four sidings, which were used for stabling excursion stock as well as goods wagons. BR Standard Class 4 4-6-0 No 75002 prepares to leave Pentrefelin with a trainload of Cuthbert seeds in the early 1960s.

The track layout at Pentrefelin has been extended by the Llangollen Railway to provide accommodation for the storage, repair and maintenance of rolling-stock. An assortment of wagons and coaches is pictured at the site on 30 September 2006, including the line's resident Class 104 diesel multiple unit. *Llangollen Railway Archive, Cuthbert Seeds/PDS*

BERWYN station had a single platform for passenger and parcels traffic, but no goods facilities. Its business declined after the Second World War and it became an unstaffed halt in 1954, with the formerly generous passenger facilities in the station house replaced by a simple wooden hut. However, the station house remained in use as a private residence long after weeds began to colonise the vacant trackbed. This was the scene in August 1977, some 12½ years after the line's closure.

The relaying of track as far as Berwyn in 1985 was a significant milestone for the Llangollen Railway Society, as it could now run a passenger service between two stations. The formal re-opening of Berwyn station was performed in June 1986 by the Society's president, His Grace The Duke of Westminster. Today the station is popular with walkers and visitors to the nearby Horseshoe Falls. Pannier tank No 6430 masquerades as 'Duck' of 'Thomas the Tank Engine' fame while hauling the 1213 departure from Carrog on 23 October 2006.

The third photograph shows tracklaying on Berwyn viaduct in 1985. *John Robinson/PDS/Peter Fisher*

BERWYN is arguably the scenic climax of today's Llangollen Railway, its station platform clinging to the steep bank of the River Dee and with distant views of the limestone crags of Eglwyseg. This was the scene in January 1966, one year after the original closure of the line. A platform extension over the viaduct had been removed some years previously.

The platform extension was restored in 2002 as part of a £400,000 scheme to recondition the viaduct, which was suffering from water penetration and needed urgent attention to allow normal trains to continue running over it. The cantilevered structure is pictured on 31 December 2005, with Prairie tank No 5199 hauling the 1300 'Mince Pie Special' from Llangollen to Carrog.

The inset shows a plaque on Berwyn station celebrating the completion of the project. *David Mitchell/PDS (2)*

GLYNDYFRDWY: Between Berwyn and Glyndyfrdwy the railway follows the bends of the river valley while the A5 road takes a straighter and more southerly course. Heading east on 2 August 1959 is an unidentified Pannier tank with a mixed goods working, conveying two of the then new 'Presflo' cement tanks as well as assorted wooden- and steel-bodied open wagons.

Passing the same spot on 23 October 2006 is a DMU formation with car No M50528 nearest the camera, playing the role of 'Daisy' on the 1200 Llangollen to Carrog service. The changes to the rural landscape are typical of those that have affected much of Britain over the past 40 years: a smaller land area is now farmed more intensively – in this case with sheep – than it used to be, while the less fertile land higher up the hillside has been abandoned and is turning into secondary woodland. A new bungalow has appeared in the middle distance. *Kevin Lane collection/PDS*

GLYNDYFRDWY: 'Manor' Class 4-6-0s Nos 7827 *Lydham Manor* and 7819 *Hinton Manor* drift towards Glyndyfrdwy with the 'Festiniog Railway Special' to Porthmadog on Saturday 20 April 1963. This was the year in which the infamous Beeching Report appeared and the fate of the Ruabon-Barmouth line would soon be sealed.

The Llangollen Railway completed tracklaying as far as Glyndyfrdwy in 1991 and regular services from Llangollen to Glyndyfrdwy began in the following year. Class 20 diesel-electric No D8142 approaches the station with the 1400 service from Llangollen to Carrog on 3 June 2006. The tree in the middle of the picture has changed little in 43 years, but new tree growth has obscured the view of the buildings near the station. *Geoff Plumb/PDS*

GLYNDYFRDWY station produced only modest revenue from passengers, though the adjacent goods yard – out of sight beyond the crossing in this photograph – was once a busy loading point for slate. The 24-lever signal box on the up platform was manned throughout the day because it controlled the crossing; it worked to either Deeside or Llangollen Goods Line Junction in the east and to either Carrog or Corwen in the west.

After the line closed, little time was wasted in removing the platforms and demolishing the buildings, with the notable exception of the station house, which survived in domestic ownership. New platforms were constructed on the old foundations, while a new site was chosen for the signal box, which was imported from Leaton. The station and signal box received the Ian Allan National Railway Heritage Award in 1995. The delightful station

CARROG: 5700 Class 0-6-0 Pannier tank No 9752 enters Carrog station with the 4.00pm train from Ruabon to Bala on 13 May 1961. Although it controlled the passing loop and two goods sidings, Carrog signal box was often switched out during the middle part of the day, leaving a single-line section between Glyndyfrdwy and Corwen.

The goal of extending the rails from Glyndyfrdwy to Carrog was achieved in 1996, giving the Llangollen Railway a 7½-mile route. The signal box is an impressively faithful copy of the original, which was demolished after the line's closure. Making a steamy entrance on 1 May 2006 is 2800 Class 2-8-0 No 3802 with the 1100 departure from Llangollen. No 3802 had only recently been returned to service, some 21 years after it was rescued from the scrapyard and 40 years since its withdrawal by BR. *Bryan Wilson, courtesy of The Transport*

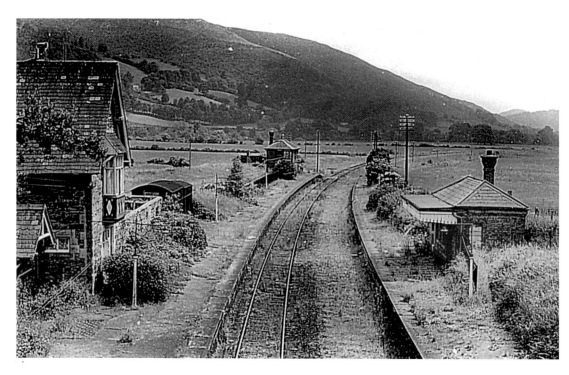

CARROG station in the mid-1960s presents a sad scene that was replicated throughout Britain in the wake of the Beeching Report. A government edict at that time required the track of closed lines to be left in place for three years after closure, but once that time was up the track removal teams usually moved in quickly. Meanwhile the replacement Crosville bus service between Ruabon and Barmouth became reputedly one of the biggest loss-makers in the region.

The transformation from dereliction to vibrancy is striking as 'Manor' Class 4-6-0 No 7822 *Foxcote Manor* arrives with the 1100 service from Llangollen on 3 June 2006. The station house at Carrog survived the 1964 closure and was bought by a member of the Llangollen Railway Trust ahead of the re-opening of the railway. Today the building houses a welcoming café, while the goods yard contains a variety of historic rolling-stock including a Full Brake coach now used as a shop. *C. L. Caddy/PDS*

Carrog to Bala Junction

BONWM was one of a number of small halts on the Ruabon to Barmouth line opened by the GWR in the 1920s in an attempt to win new traffic. It consisted of a simple platform just over 70 feet in length with a wooden shelter, nameboard and electric lamp. Although it served a sparsely populated rural area and can never have generated much business, Bonwm remained open until the closure of the line in December 1964.

The vacant trackbed at Bonwm is pictured on 23 October 2006. Some clearance work has taken place to prepare for track relaying between Carrog and Corwen, which in all likelihood will mark the final stage of the Llangollen Railway's expansion. The A5 road seen in the 'past' picture is as busy as ever but now shrouded from the trackbed by trees. *Lens of Sutton collection/WPS*

CORWEN was a busy market town and had the largest intermediate station on the Ruabon to Barmouth line. Its importance was boosted by the LNWR line from Ruthin and Denbigh, which joined GWR metals at the east end of the station. 4300 Class 2-6-0 No 6367 arrives with the 3.45pm Ruabon to Pwllheli service on 13 August 1953. The passenger service from Ruthin had been withdrawn earlier that year and the nameboard on the down platform shows a blank space where the connection would once have been advertised.

Traces of the east end of the down platform were still visible when the site was revisited on 1 May 2006. But the Llangollen Railway will not be able to extend its rails here, because a sewage works occupies part of the alignment just east of the former station. Instead the railway plans a new terminus on the outskirts of the town.
H. C. Casserley/PDS

CORWEN: The substantial brick buildings on the down platform comprised a booking hall, booking office, parcels office, Station Master's office, District Inspector's office, guards' room, general waiting room, ladies' waiting room, refreshment rooms, various store rooms and two lavatories. In pre-nationalisation days some of the station staff were employed jointly by the LMS and the GWR. The frontage is pictured on 15 July 1963, with a distinctly older car parked prominently in front of the entrance.

The location is instantly recognisable today, more than four decades after the last train departed. A showroom for Ifor Williams Trailers occupies the surviving building, which appears to be well maintained, while a typical selection of early-21st-century cars can be seen on the forecourt. *R. M. Casserley/PDS*

CORWEN: A footbridge at the west end of the station provided the vantage for this view of BR Standard 4-6-0 No 75027 arriving with the 1.20pm Chester to Barmouth service on 15 July 1963. The unusual ridge-and-furrow-pattern awning on the down platform is seen to good effect, while Corwen East signal box is partly hidden by the brick shelter on the up platform. The goods and engine servicing facilities at Corwen were located behind the photographer on the west side of the town.

Trailers of varying shapes and sizes occupy the west end of former station site on 1 May 2006. No 75027 has been preserved and is based on the Bluebell Railway. *R. M. Casserley/PDS*

CORWEN: BR Standard 4-6-0 No 75021 approaches Corwen from the west with a four-coach train bound for Ruabon on 28 August 1964. The signal above the leading coach was the home signal for Corwen West, while the siding in the foreground was the shunting neck for the station goods yard.

The railway alignment west of Corwen is now in use as a footpath, but the trackbed at this point is hidden by conifers, as pictured on 30 September 2006. *Derek Cross/PDS*

CYNWYD: A handful of passengers greet the arrival of 5700 Class Pannier tank No 3749 with an eastbound train on 2 August 1962. The station only ever had a single platform, although room appears to have been left for a potential second track and platform on the right. Two ground frames controlled access to the goods sidings, which appear to be empty. The goods warehouse was partly demolished shortly after the date of the photograph, but the yard remained officially open for goods until the summer of 1964.

The same view on 30 September 2006 shows no traces of the railway, although the rotten remains of a wooden gate were found at the top of the former station approach road. *H. B. Priestley, David Southern collection/PDS*

LLANDRILLO station is pictured facing east on 25 August 1962, with no obvious sign of life either on the platforms or in the modest single-tracked goods yard. The ensemble of buildings would have changed little since the railway first opened in the 1860s, but soon the tracks would be gone for ever in this part of rural Merionethshire.

Although the platforms have disappeared, the railway alignment is still traceable as it passes through a busy timber yard. The 'present' photograph is dated 30 September 2006. *P. J. Garland collection/PDS*

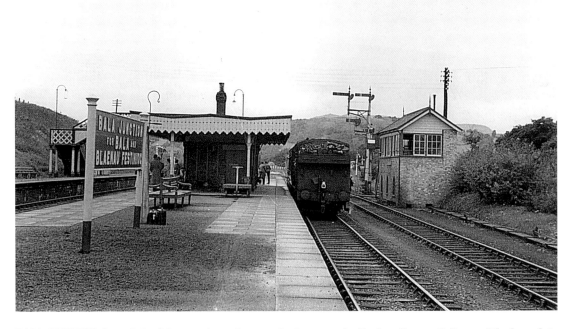

BALA JUNCTION: Intended solely as an interchange point between the Ruabon-Barmouth line and the branch to Bala and Blaenau Ffestiniog, Bala Junction station had no road access and was included only as a footnote in the public timetable. Nevertheless it was a busy railway location, with three platform roads and a run-round loop. This was the scene facing west on 15 August 1953, with 7400 Class Pannier tank No 7443 standing at the island platform with the Bala branch service.

More than half a century after closure, on 16 September 2006, it is still possible to walk along the island platform, now lightly grazed by sheep from the surrounding fields. *H. C. Casserley/PDS*

BALA JUNCTION station is pictured facing east on 16 April 1958, showing the 53-lever signal box, two water columns and four electric token posts – all essential features of everyday operations in the steam era. Bala Junction had no goods facilities, but passengers awaiting connections were provided with waiting rooms and toilets on the island platform.

The platform edge is still a prominent feature of the scene in the 'present' photograph dated 16 September 2006. *H. B. Priestley, Pacer Archive collection/PDS*

BALA JUNCTION: 4300 Class 2-6-0 No 6311 comes off the Bala branch at Bala Junction with a long mixed goods working in the late 1950s. The GWR provided two bi-directional tracks between Bala and Bala Junction: one was the main line worked by electric token, and the other was the relief line, which could be used by local movements without drawing a token. Just above the locomotive is the two-span bridge over the River Dee; it was the position of the river that prevented the Ruabon-Barmouth line from passing through Bala itself.

The river bridge was removed after the line closed but the alignment of the former main line to Barmouth is still clearly visible today. Just west of the former station the trackbed is occupied by a scrapyard. This was the scene on 16 September 2006. *C. L. Caddy collection/PDS*

The Bala Lake Railway

Trains first came to this quiet land in 1868, when a cross-country railway was opened to link the industrial borderlands with the Cambrian coastal resorts around Barmouth. The line from Bala Junction to Dolgelley (Dolgellau) was built by the Bala & Dolgelley Railway Company and operated by the Great Western Railway, which absorbed the B&DR in 1877. In 1896 the GWR enlarged Llanuwchllyn station with an extended building and signal box, and a long loop and second platform were added to enable trains to pass each other. Following nationalisation in 1948, most of the railway's traffic was diverted to the former Cambrian Railway line between Welshpool and Machynlleth. Passenger services ended in 1965 and the line from Llangollen to Barmouth was closed.

Rebirth came in 1971 when a local engineer, George Barnes, with the help of the late Tom Jones CBE, formed the Bala Lake Railway Ltd (the first company to be registered in the Welsh language). Conversion to narrow gauge began in 1972, and the first 1¼ miles were opened to passengers on 13 August. In 1979 a passing loop was introduced at Llangower and the station at Llanuwchllyn was rebuilt: the original single-storey building was increased to two storeys, and a new toilet block and canopy were added to the platform side. Work continued, and the winter of 1988-89 saw improvements to the station at Bala (Penybont); the wooden platform was re-aligned and rebuilt with concrete block walling, and at the same time it was lengthened to take eight coaches.

(With thanks to the Bala Lake Railway for permission to draw from their attractive *Visitor's Guide*, available at Llanuwchllyn.)

Looking west from Llanuwchllyn station, we see the coaling and watering facilities at the end of the line being used by *Alice* **on 4 July 2006.** *JCH*

BALA LAKE HALT was originally opened in 1934 by the GWR, presumably with the intent of encouraging tourism to the area and Bala Lake in particular. The view on 21 June 1967 (looking towards Llanuwchllyn in standard gauge days) shows the short platform and basic wooden shelter.

In the 'present' view, taken on 9 August 2006, the much longer and well-built platform can be seen, together with a modern waiting shelter and run-round facility. The iron footbridge, which carries a public footpath across the line, remains in situ. *C. L. Caddy/JCH*

BALA LAKE HALT: On 2 September 1984 No 3 *Holy War* sets out for Llanuwchllyn with a well-loaded train. Built by Hunslet, it was supplied new to Dinorwic Quarries in 1902. It had the distinction of being the last steam locomotive to work in a British slate quarry, finishing at Dinorwic in 1967. After a period at Quainton Road, it came to the Bala Lake Railway at the end of 1975.

Twenty-four years later, on 4 July 2006, other than a different engine – *Alice* – and a lengthened platform, the scene is much the same, with several metal advertisements now adorning the bridge supports. *Alice* is quietly waiting for departure with her driver chatting to visitors. The loco is another built by Hunslet in the same year as *Holy War*, and now also carries the number 3, having taken it over from her sister engine. *Gavin Morrison/JCH*

BETWEEN LLANGOWER HALT AND FLAG STATION: Llangower station was opened in 1929, and lasted until closure of the line in January 1965, while Flag is known also as Glanllyn, and was originally opened as a private halt for Sir Watkin Williams-Wynn, whose home was across the lake at Glanllwyn Hall. This delightful view was taken on 2 September 1984 – *Holy War* heads east, having passed Flag station, which is out of view.

There has been considerable foliage growth, so the 'present' photo shows Llangower Halt looking west, but the spit of land that juts into the bay is in the background and connects the two pictures. *Alice* is about to leave for the Bala terminal on 4 July 2006. *Gavin Morrison/JCH*

LLANUWCHLLYN was originally known as Pandy, and opened on 1 October 1868; it was renamed to its current title by BR, and closed in January 1965, to be re-opened by the narrow-gauge Bala Lake Railway in August 1972. In the photograph of 21 June 1967, looking east, we see the atmospheric rural station with modest facilities but including a water column for the use of engines of down trains. The line was single in both directions beyond the passing loop, and only the down-side platform had an awning at that time.

In the 'present' picture of 4 July 2006, apart from the reduced gauge there have been a number of changes. This is now the HQ and principal station on the railway, and although only the original up platform is used, the down side is kept in immaculate condition. Both platform buildings now have an awning and the main building has been considerably extended. On 4 July 2006 a train is standing at the platform awaiting departure to the Bala terminus, and a bogie truck containing coal stands on the siding on the right. Behind the photographer are the coaling and watering facilities. *C. L. Caddy/JCH*

LLANUWCHLLYN: This photograph of 19 December 1964, not long before the line's closure, shows two of BR's small Standard locomotives, designed by Ivatt, which became stalwarts on many rural lines. On the left is 2MT 2-6-0 tender version No 46446 (allocated to Machynlleth), which was much photographed on the line, with 'sister' 2-6-2 tank version, No 41204 (a Croes Newydd engine), on the right. One of the crew is about to pass the single-line token to the signalman waiting on the platform, who will then hand it on to the up train on the other platform.

Apart from the principal change to narrow gauge, the main difference is that the down platform is no longer in use. *Alice* has run round her train and is about to re-couple before departure east to Bala on 4 July 2006. In the background are the buildings used by the railway for servicing and restoration work. *Gavin Morrison/JCH*

LLANUWCHLLYN: On 30 May 1978 *Maid Marian* is seen arriving from Bala with a fully loaded train. When built by Hunslet in 1903 this engine had a large brass dome, but at some later time was rebuilt with a standard domeless boiler. She came to Bala in 1975, having seen service on the Llanberis Lake Railway, at Bressingham Gardens in Norfolk, and her original home at Port Dinorwic. Note the bags of coal at the platform end.

More than 27 years later there have been changes to the buildings on the left and modifications to the signals, but basically the view is much the same, although taken from platform level. No 3 *Holy War* is disappearing into the distance in early December 2005. *Brian Morrison/JCH*

Llanuwchllyn to Barmouth

LLYS HALT was opened by the GWR in June 1934 and consisted of a single wood-edged platform on the down side of the line. Looking east from the crossing, the 'past' photo of 25 August 1962 shows the whole platform and the rather poor shelter. The station came under the care of the Station Master at Llanuwchllyn, and closed in 1965.

In the 'present' shot the house, which can be seen behind the imposing gates, bears the name of 'Llys Arthur' ('Arthur's Court'). The line of the track curves away to the left towards Llanuwchllyn. *P. J. Garland, courtesy of Roger Carpenter/JCH*

GARNEDDWEN HALT: Beyond the station towards Dolgellau the line crossed the main Bala-Dolgellau Road, and it was from there that this photo of Ivatt 2-6-0 2MT No 46446 was taken on Saturday 19 December 1964, slowing for the stop at Garneddwen Halt with an eastbound train.

The outline of the Aran ridge still defines the location on 23 October 2006. The cutting that once carried the railway is heavily overgrown. *Dave Mitchell/PDS*

50

GARNEDDWEN HALT, just before the summit of the line, was opened by the GWR in July 1928, and survived until the line closure in January 1965. In 1913 a loop had been added in order to shorten the section between Llanuwchllyn and Drws-y-Nant. The platforms were staggered, and were reached by a path across a field from the Bala to Dolgellau road. There was a low population in the area, and had there not been the necessity of a loop passing place, the station would probably never have been built. On 19 December 1964 Ivatt 2MT 2-6-2T No 41204 pulls away from the station, which can be seen beyond with the signal box on the right, en route towards Drws-y-Nant.

In our 'present' picture of 2 August 2006, more than 40 years later, it is remarkable that the site of the station is still to be seen, with a few rotting remains of a platform. As is so often the case, the rail alignment is clearly seen from the line of trees. *Gavin Morrison/JCH*

51

DRWS-Y-NANT was one of the oldest stations on the line, having been opened by the Bala & Dolgelley (sic) Railway in October 1868, later to be absorbed into the GWR. Looking west, again on 19 December 1964, BR Standard 2-6-0 No 46446 approaches the station with a two-coach train to Bala and Llangollen. As can be seen, this was also a passing place with a short siding on the left-hand side, the line continuing single-track to the west.

After the closure the adjacent main road between Bala and Dolgellau was upgraded and widened, taking in part of the old railway alignment. Looking west on 7 November 2006, the Station House remains in use as a private dwelling, on the left-hand side of where the line ran. Behind the photographer, looking towards Bala, the remains of the station platforms can still be seen. *Gavin Morrison/JCH*

BONT NEWYDD was opened by the B&D in August 1868, a little earlier than Drws-y-Nant, and survived until closure of the line in 1965. In 1923 a loop was added to make it a passing point. The signal box stood by the crossing of the minor road to Brithdir, and as seen in the picture of 25 August 1962 the station was very basic with a shelter on the down side, and a small booking office, waiting room, etc, on the up side, visible beyond the lady waiting by the roadside.

Today nothing remains, but the road sign to Brithdir makes a good point of reference between the two photographs. There has been considerable growth of foliage, and it seems that the wall has been demolished, now just a grass verge. *P. J. Garland collection/JCH*

DOLSERAU HALT: This tiny and lonely platform had a relatively short life, opened by the GWR in February 1935 and closed by BR in October 1951. The nameboard stated 'Dolserau Halt for Torrent Walk', a nearby tourist attraction. In the 'past' photo of June 1949 a single passenger awaits her train.

The site is close by the river, but is now completely surrounded by tree growth as can be seen in the photograph of 4 July 2006. *R. M. Casserley collection/JCH*

DOLGELLAU: On 30 July 1964 BR Standard 2-6-0 Ivatt 2MT No 46446 has just come into the station from the sidings with two coaches forming the 1341 train to Barmouth, which will call at Penmaenpool, Arthog and Barmouth Junction (subsequently Morfa Mawddach).

Following the closure of the line, the track alignment formed the basis of a town by-pass. Looking from the bridge over the new road leading to the town centre on 4 July 2006 there is nothing to be seen of the railway whatsoever. *Geoff Plumb/JCH*

DOLGELLAU, formerly Dolgelley, was one of the most important stations on the line, having been opened by the Bala & Dolgelly (yet another spelling!) Railway on 4 August 1868, followed in June of the following year by the Aberystwyth & Welch (sic) Coast Railway, which closed almost immediately on 1 August. At Dolgellau the GWR line from Ruabon came to an end, and there was an end-on junction with the Cambrian Railways, which had constructed the line from Barmouth Junction as far as Penmaenpool, when funds had run out, and it was not until 1869 that it was completed to Dolgellau. The Cambrian buildings were on the down side and those of the GWR on the up. The 'past' photo shows the signal box and Ivatt 2-6-0 No 46521 with a two-coach train awaiting departure.

Once again, but looking in the opposite direction from the previous page, the railway has completely disappeared, although the alignment is still apparent. *J. A. Peden/JCH*

PENMAENPOOL: In June 1964 Ivatt 2MT 2-6-0 46446 is at the head of a two-coach Barmouth-Dolgellau service, passing the George Hotel.

Today's view is almost identical, though taken on 24 July 2006, 42 years later. The alignment remains precisely the same, but the hotel has become the 'George III Hotel'. At some point a semaphore signal has been added just in front of the hotel as a nice touch to remind us of the railway. *Derek Cross/JCH*

PENMAENPOOL: Ex-GWR 4300 Class 2-6-0 No 7341 leaves the station with a Chester-Barmouth service in August 1960. The wooden platform is clear to see, as is the siding on the right of the down platform.

Today the whole area of the station is a nicely laid-out car park for the many visitors, as seen on 24 July 2006.
Derek Cross/JCH

PENMAENPOOL: This view again shows the George Hotel with the track running immediately in front – whether this would have been considered 'safe' today is doubtful. On the left-hand side can be seen the road toll bridge that crosses the estuary and saves a few miles on the Dolgellau-Barmouth route. The station building is just beyond the hotel and the up platform further on.

By 4 July 2006 there has been little change apart from the removal of the track. The signal is undoubtedly of GWR style and beyond it can be seen the signal box, which was by the platform; the box, opened in 1936 and closed in January 1965, has been preserved and is currently occupied by the RSPB. *Courtesy of Mrs Gwyneth Williams/JCH*

PENMAENPOOL is such a beautiful and tranquil place that it is hard to believe that it was once the home of a small engine shed, which was a sub-shed to Croes Newydd; the allocation was often one 0-4-2T (supplied by Machynlleth) for the Dolgellau-Barmouth 'auto-train', and at least one other loco from Croes Newydd stayed overnight. It was a wooden building of the '2TS' dead-ended type, south of the line and west of the station. In the photo of 18 October 1964 we see two BR-built locos – Ivatt 2-6-0 No 46446 on the left and 4-6-0 4MT No 75023 on the right.

The shed closed in January 1965, and although it still stood as late as 1975, it was subsequently demolished. In the 'present' picture, taken on 24 July 2006, it can be seen that there has been the usual growth of trees, etc, but the building beyond the shed remains, with a new house built on this side of it. The path is part of the

ARTHOG station's lifespan was from March 1870 (Cambrian Railways) to January 1965 (British Railways), with the Great Western in between. Today it is a remarkably rural place, approached either by a gated road off the Penmaenpool to Tywyn road, or by walking along the Mawddach Trail. One can only wonder what it was like in 1870, when it can be reasonably assumed that the local population was very low. Looking towards Morfa Mawddach we can see the whole station beyond the road crossing, with its waiting room and lamps.

Today nothing remains of the station, as seen in the picture of 9 August 2006. The wide path is part of the Mawddach Trail, which begins way back at Dolgellau and leads to Morfa Mawddach and across the bridge to Barmouth. The scene shows the amount of tree growth, but the hills beyond remain the same.

The nameboard from the station was saved and is mounted above a garage by the nearby main road.
David Southern collection/JCH (2)

BARMOUTH JUNCTION, originally a terminus before the completion of Barmouth Bridge, was opened by the Aberystwyth & Welch Coast Railway in July 1865. Once the bridge was open, passengers for Barmouth were conveyed by horse and carriage until it was approved for rail use. Additionally, the triangle could be used for turning engines if the turntable at Barmouth was too small. An Ivatt 2-6-0 at the head of the usual two-coach train leaves the station for Barmouth on 29 June 1964. The train has come from Dolgellau, and the line from Dovey Junction is in the left foreground, forming the northern junction of the triangle.

The station was re-named by BR as Morfa Mawddach in 1960 and remains open today, although the line to Dolgellau was closed in 1965. On 24 July 2006 Class 158 No 158829 passes the station forming the 0907 service from Machynlleth to Pwllheli, not having stopped as the station is a 'Request' stop. *Dave Mitchell/JCH*

BARMOUTH BRIDGE had to be closed for a period when the woodwork was attacked by a marine worm, but following full refurbishment it survives. On 2 June 1978, prior to closure, a Class 108 DMU, forming the 1042 Shrewsbury-Pwllheli service, crosses the estuary, showing the full length of the bridge from the north bank. Cader Idris lies brooding in the background.

Arriva Wales ran steam specials from the end of July to the end of August in 2006. On 9 August BR Standard 4MT 2-6-0 No 76079 is seen crossing the bridge en route from Machynlleth to Porthmadog. There are now no facilities to turn the engine so it had to run tender-first on the down run. It is most unusual in a 'Past and Present' title for the 'past' to be a DMU and the 'present' a steam loco! *Brian Morrison/JCH*

BARMOUTH BRIDGE: On 7 June 1963 BR Standard 3MT 2-6-2T No 82003 (allocated to Machynlleth) has just crossed the bridge with its three coaches; the origin of the train is most likely to have been Dolgellau.

Forty-three years later, on 9 August 2006, No 76079's seven-coach train is almost over the bridge. There is very little difference in the two pictures other than the small culvert on the left, which has been replaced by a more modern structure, and the new roof on the building in the centre, which is by the toll booth (for pedestrians). *T. J. Edgington/JCH*

BARMOUTH station was opened in June 1867 by the Aberystwyth & Welch Coast Railway, later to become part of the Cambrian Railways and, in turn, the GWR. Until the line from Dolgellau to Barmouth Junction closed in 1965, there was access from three directions, north from Pwllheli, west from Dolgellau and beyond, and south from Dovey Junction, giving the option of Aberystwyth or Machynlleth. With the closure of the Dolgellau line, the route to Bala, Llangollen and the GWR main line was no longer available. On 23 July 1962 two ex-GWR locos head south, having just passed through Barmouth station. 4-6-0 No 7820 *Dinmore Manor* (since preserved at the West Somerset Railway) is the nearer of the two, coupled to an unidentified 4300 Class 2-6-0. To the left can be seen the Excursion platform, which was also used by the shuttle service to and from Dolgellau.

There have been considerable changes by 9 August 2006. The line has been singled, with just a passing place at the station. A Class 158 approaches forming the 1100 from Machynlleth to Pwllheli. Barmouth South signal box (now preserved on the Llangollen Railway) stood on the south side of the crossing on the west side of the line; nearby a small plaque commemorates the box. All trains stop until the barriers come down before proceeding into the station. There is nothing left of the Excursion platform, but the building on the left remains, now in use as Theatr y Ddraig (Dragon Theatre), converted from a Victorian chapel. *Dave Mitchell/ JCH(2)*

Mae'r plac hwn yn dynodi safle
Bocs Signal Rheilffordd Y Cambrian
Adeiladwyd - 1883 Tynnwyd i lawr - 1999

This plaque marks the site where
the Cambrian Railway Signal Box once stood
Erected - 1883 Dismantled - 1999

BARMOUTH: BR Ivatt 2-6-0 No 78005 has arrived at the Excursion platform with the shuttle from Dolgellau and is about to run round its train. Note the loading gauge.

There has been little change in the buildings in the background, although the Excursion platform and shelter, and the footbridge crossing the line by the station have gone, and of course the line has been reduced to a single track, except through the station. Two-car Class 158 No 158851 enters the station forming the 0905 service from Machynlleth to Pwllheli. *T. J. Edgington/JCH*

The Fairbourne Railway

When the Cambrian Coast railway opened in 1865, Barmouth Viaduct had not been completed, so a temporary halt was opened at Morfa Henddol (which later became Fairbourne), and passengers wishing to travel to Barmouth were conveyed by horse-drawn bus to the ferry. This arrangement ended after two years when the bridge was completed.

The first line linking Fairbourne to the Barmouth ferry at Penrhyn Point was a 2-foot-gauge horse-drawn tramway opened by Mr McDougall, of flour company fame. The purpose was to convey building materials from a brickworks and from the Cambrian Railways to a series of private housing developments. By the turn of the century the tramway had begun to carry passengers, and continued to do so until the outbreak of the First World War, remaining exclusively horse-worked. The name Fairbourne was decided upon by Mr McDougall and the Cambrian Railways.

In 1916 ownership passed to Narrow Gauge Railways Ltd. This company had been formed to promote and construct 15-inch-gauge railways, and the Fairbourne line proved suitable for just such a conversion. In 1923 the line was leased to the Barmouth Motor Boat & Ferry Company, but the following year brought another change of ownership when it passed to the Fairbourne Estate & Development Company. In 1940 the line was closed for the duration of the Second World War, but by 1946 had new owners.

During the next 20 years many improvements were made, the principal one being the development of the Fairbourne terminus complex, with provision made for colour light signalling, replacement of the permanent way, and the appearance of new locomotives. The 1950s and '60s were the zenith of the railway in its 15-inch guise, but in the 1970s and early '80s it suffered from falling passenger numbers, partly because more people were travelling overseas for holidays and there was increased competition from other railways in Wales.

In the late 1970s a 12¼-inch-gauge railway was constructed in Brittany, and was considered an ideal gauge. The owner was a Mr Ellerton, who had family connections at Fairbourne. It followed that in 1984 a new company was formed, the North Wales Narrow Gauge Railways Ltd, which bought the railway in the early part of 1984. At the end of that year there was reconstruction at Fairbourne terminus, and re-gauging began at the end of the 1985 season. The following year the other terminus at Barmouth Ferry was extensively altered, with a new building containing a café, and the track configuration was changed. In 1990 the Ellerton family put the railway up for sale, but a buyer was not found until 1995. The new owners, Mr & Mrs Melton and Professor & Mrs Atkinson, had taken possession of the railway by Easter of that year, and a new company was formed – North Wales Coast Light Railway – which has continued to operate the railway ever since.

Towards the end of 2006 it was announced that the railway would no longer be the Fairbourne & Barmouth Steam Railway and would revert to using the name 'The Fairbourne Railway' so as to avoid passengers expecting the line to run across the Mawddach Estuary rather than connecting with the ferry service at Barmouth Ferry station.

(Thanks to the railway for permission to quote freely from their excellent fully-illustrated souvenir guide book available at Fairbourne and Barmouth Ferry.)

The Stout Director, who greeted everyone on the 'Friendly Engine Day' of 24 July 2006. *JCH*

FAIRBOURNE: On 2 September 1984 No 362 *Sea Train* is seen prior to departure for Barmouth Ferry. This 2-4-2 had been known as *Siân* and was re-styled to resemble a US-type locomotive with the name of *Sydney*.

The 'past' picture was taken just before the re-modelling of the terminus, and today's picture shows the conversion of the former departure area into the locomotive shed. The centre track can still be seen on the 31 August 2005, although it cannot now be used. *Gavin Morrison/JCH*

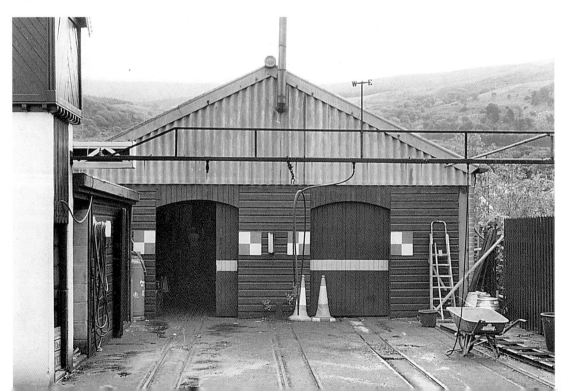

FAIRBOURNE: This view of 2-4-2 *Katie* was taken on 27 August 1984; built in 1950 by G&S Light Engineering, she is now at Windmill Farm Railway in Lancashire. She has a decidedly GWR look about her!

The present-day view shows the complete changes that have taken place, although the buildings to the left and the hillsides beyond connect the two pictures. *Beddgelert* and *Sherpa* are ready to take the first train of the day; the former is an 0-6-4ST built in 1979, and the latter an 0-4-0ST based on the Darjeeling & Himalayan Railway Sharp Stewart type. The 'face' on the front of *Beddgelert* tells all – it was a 'Friendly Engine Day'! *N. R. Knight/JCH*

FAIRBOURNE: This earlier photograph, taken on 7 August 1973, shows *Siân* leaving for Barmouth Ferry before conversion – she was barely recognisable when she became No 362.

There have been so many changes that only the hillside behind and the top of the house just visible in the centre of the photograph provide links between the 'past' and 'present' on 24 July 2006. *Yeo* has just arrived from Penrhyn Point; this 2-6-2T was built by David Curwen in 1978 and was based on the Lynton & Barnstaple Manning Wardle type. Painted in Southern malachite green, it was originally called *Jubilee*. *Roger Siviter/JCH*

GOLF HALT: Formerly known as Gorsaffawddachhaidraiganheddogleddollonpenrhynareudraethceredigion, the station once laid claim to the longest station name, not only in Wales, ahead of Llanfair PG, but in the world! Translated, it meant 'The Mawddach Station with its dragon's teeth on the northerly Penrhyn drive on the golden beach of Cardigan Bay'. On 8 August 1973 *Katie* makes her way towards Barmouth Ferry, about a third of the way from Fairbourne terminus.

Nearly 33 years later, on 24 July 2006, *Beddgelert*, wears its 'Friendly Engine' face, is at the head of seven coaches. A few buildings have been added to the background, but the changes are very few. *Roger Siviter/JCH*

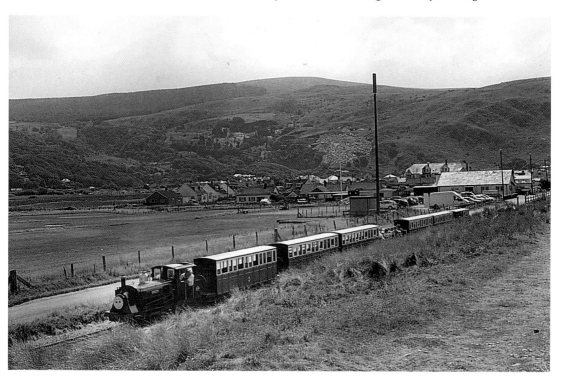

BEACH HALT is the first station along the line to Barmouth Ferry, and on 2 September 1984 No 362 is seen steaming gently along. Nearly 21 years later, on 31 August 2005, the scene is virtually unchanged as *Sherpa* runs through en route for the Ferry. *Gavin Morrison/JCH*

BARMOUTH FERRY: On 27 August 1984 No 362 *Sydney* leaves the terminus, with Barmouth Bridge visible in the background.

Subsequently there has been a re-alignment of the track, as seen on 24 July 2006, with *Beddgelert* running round its train – the bridge is again clearly seen in the distance. *N. R. Knight/JCH*

BARMOUTH FERRY (Ferry terminal): This wonderful old photograph of circa 1899 shows the horse tram carrying passengers at the end of the line. In the background can be seen the east end of Barmouth.

Nearly a century later the view remains much the same, with the row of houses and of course the permanent backdrop of the hills behind the town. On 27 August 1984 No 362 is about to return to Fairbourne.

The 'present' picture shows *Beddgelert* coupling up before departure for Fairbourne on 24 July 2006. In the span of more than 100 years the background is much the same. New buildings have been built by the station, including a café and toilets. Passengers can take the ferry across the estuary to Barmouth. *Bill Hyde collection/N. R. Knight/JCH*

Bala to Blaenau Ffestiniog

BALA: Standing in front of the crenellated goods warehouse just east of Bala Town station on 15 August 1953 is 5700 Class Pannier tank No 5742 with a mixed goods train. The unusual design of the warehouse was due to pressure from a local landowner who objected to the railway's construction on aesthetic grounds. In its heyday the goods depot handled large quantities of livestock as well as coal and general goods for local distribution. The view faces east, and the in the distance can be seen the two tracks curving round towards Bala Junction.

On 16 September 2006 a visit to the same location finds no trace of the former railway, now superseded by an industrial estate. *H. C. Casserley/PDS*

BALA: 1400 Class 0-4-2T No 5811 stands at the two-platform Bala station with two red and cream coaches in this mid-1950s scene. The locomotive's allocation plate shows 84J, which was the code for Croes Newydd – including the sub-sheds at Bala, Penmaenpool and Trawsfynydd – until it changed to 89B in January 1961. The modest locomotive servicing facilities at Bala were located on the north side of the line just east of the station, opposite the goods yard.

The pine trees that were a feature of many GWR stations in North Wales are still standing in the 'present' view of 16 September 2006, having outlived the railway by more than four decades. *Lens of Sutton collection/PDS*

77

BALA: A busy scene at Bala on 29 March 1959: 7400 Class Pannier tank No 7428 comes off a train that has just arrived from Blaenau Ffestiniog, while 5700 Class Pannier tank No 8727 waits to take over for the short journey to Bala Junction, connecting with a train to Ruabon or Barmouth. Less than a year after the date of this photograph the passenger service between Bala and Blaenau Ffestiniog would be withdrawn, leaving Bala station to eke out its remaining years as a terminus.

Nothing but the distant hillside remains to link the 'past' picture with the 'present' scene dated 23 October 2006. Trains of a different kind are waiting to play their part in an autumn funfair. *Gavin Morrison/PDS*

BALA: Looking north from the road overbridge just north of Bala station in the spring of 1961, Pannier tank No 9752 runs round its train on the stump of the then recently closed line to Blaenau Ffestiniog. The railway allotments appear well tended.

The alignment of the track can still be traced in the 'present' photograph dated 9 August 2006. A wooden gate in the centre of the picture has outlived the closure of railway by more than three decades. *David Mitchell/JCH*

FRONGOCH was the first station on the line from Bala to Blaenau Ffestiniog, opened by the Bala & Blaenau Ffestiniog Railway in 1882 and backed by the GWR. Although serving a rural hamlet, the station had a Station Master's house, booking office, waiting room, etc, with a platform-mounted signal box, as seen in the photograph of 15 August 1953. There was a siding with run-round facility beyond the single platform on the Ffestiniog side. The station remained open to passengers until January 1960 and to freight for a further 12 months. In the foreground can be seen the electric token exchange apparatus.

In the 'present' pictures of 9 August 2006, the signal box remains virtually intact, and immediately beyond is the Station Master's house, now a private dwelling. *H. C. Casserley/JCH (2)*

ARENIG was said to be one of the bleakest stations on the whole of the GWR system, located 1,135 feet above sea level. Opened by the Bala & Ffestiniog Railway in 1865, it lasted until closed to passengers in 1960, and closed completely in 1961. It must have been a lonely place with a very small local community, but in 1908 the opening of the Arenig Granite Company's quarry brought previously unknown activity, as the products from the quarry (ballast, roadstone, etc) were distributed by rail. The station was a passing place with platforms on both sides and a loop siding through the stone-crushing plant, as well as an overhead conveyor system from the quarry, which brought the stone to be crushed. Looking towards Blaenau, we can see the up platform with the crushing plant on the right-hand side. It is probable that this photograph was taken from the guard's van of one of the last goods trains to use the line, the final one being on 27 January 1961.

Today there is very little to show of either the station or the quarry. In the photograph of 2 August 2006 the far hills match the 'past' photo, while on the left-hand side can be seen the remains of the supports for the conveyor belt. *Neville Knight/JCH*

CWM PRYSOR HALT was opened by the Bala & Ffestiniog Railway in 1902, and marked the summit of the line, some 1,278 feet above sea level. Its single windswept platform provided a lifeline for a handful of local people working on nearby hill farms and fishermen visiting Llyn Tryweryn. A passing loop was built on the Blaenau Ffestiniog side of the halt in 1906-08, but closed just after the Second World War. The decaying but still functional passenger platform is pictured, looking north, from a passing train on 15 August 1953. The remains of the former loop, now reduced to a refuge siding, can be seen beyond the platform.

Today the A4212 road occupies a short stretch of the former trackbed as it skirts Llyn Tryweryn. Commercial forestry has transformed the surrounding countryside, as seen on 16 September 2006. *R. M. Casserley/PDS*

LLAFAR HALT was another remote outpost on the Bala to Blaenau Ffestiniog line, perched in an unlikely position above the Prysor valley about 1½ miles east of Trawsfynydd. It was opened by the GWR in 1932 and had no facilities other than a very basic platform and shelter, as pictured in this west-facing view of 20 March 1959. Between 1930 and 1934 the GWR opened a total of six halts between Bala and Blaenau Ffestiniog in an attempt to increase its meagre volumes of passenger traffic. Despite the initiative the line was to close before publication of the Beeching Report, with passenger services finishing in January 1960 and goods just over a year later.

A pleasant – in fine weather! – public footpath traces the railway alignment past the long-forgotten site of Llafar Halt on 16 September 2006. *R. M. Casserley/PDS*

TRAWSFYNYDD: Marking the end of the descent from Cwm Prysor, Trawsfynydd was one of the more important intermediate stations on the Bala to Blaenau Ffestiniog line. It still boasts its full range of facilities in this scene dated 16 August 1957, although the bricked-up window on the up platform shelter is one of the more obvious signs that decline had already set in. The goods warehouse beyond the station appears to be still in use, but the cattle dock platform in front of it is grassed over. The body of an old clerestory coach can just be seen behind the signal box.

Today the station building is a private house and the former trackbed is a carefully tended lawn, while the former goods shed survives in industrial use. *H. B. Priestley, Pacer Archive collection/PDS*

Troops landing Station, Trawsfynydd.

TRAWSFYNYDD MILITARY STATION: In 1903 artillery ranges were opened near Trawsfynydd, producing a welcome influx of business for the railway. From 1911 that traffic was handled at a separate two-platform station, located on the other side of the road overbridge from the main station. This fascinating scene shows two GWR saddle tank locomotives at the head of a typical military train of the First World War era, comprising clerestory coaches for the soldiers, flat wagons for the guns, and horse-boxes for the animals. A substantial fence shields the station from the main running line to Blaenau Ffestiniog.

The military traffic had fizzled out by the 1950s and the station was then abandoned. However, a visit on 16 September 2006 found the platforms still very much in evidence. *John Ryan collection/PDS*

TRAWSFYNYDD: In the early 1960s BR adapted a siding beside the former Trawsfynydd Lake Halt as a railhead for flasks to and from Trawsfynydd nuclear power station. Equipped with a Goliath overhead crane, the siding came into use in 1964 when the line from Trawsfynydd to Blaenau Ffestiniog was re-opened and connected to the former LNWR Conwy Valley line. Assorted Central Electricity Generating Board staff oversee the transfer of a flask from an FNA wagon on 17 April 1985.

Regular flask trains to Trawsfynydd ceased in 1995 and the last working took place in April 1997, since when the loading terminal has gradually become hidden under brambles and saplings. The site is pictured on 16 September 2006. *Both PDS*

MAENTWROG ROAD station served the villages of Gellilydan, Maentwrog and Tanybwlch. On 16 August 1957 7400 Class Pannier tank No 7442 calls with the 11.55 service from Bala to Blaenau Ffestiniog. The wording on the station nameboard – 'MAENTWROG ROAD FOR TANYBWLCH DISTANCE 3 MILES' – makes it absolutely clear that passengers must expect a long walk. The station only ever had a single platform for passengers; however, it was also equipped with goods facilities including a run-round loop on the other side of the road overbridge, behind the photographer in this view.

More than two decades after closure, the surviving station buildings and platform set the scene for Class 25 No 25058 as it hauls a single flask from Trawsfynydd on 17 April 1985. The skyline is dominated by the power station itself, then just over 20 years old and destined to supply power to the national grid for another decade.

In the third photograph, dated 16 September 2006, the former station building has been smartened up and extended, while trees overshadow the now disused branch line. The power station is also now disused but still a dominant feature of the landscape.
H. B. Priestley, Pacer Archive collection/PDS (2)

FESTINIOG: 1400 Class 0-4-2T No 5810 enters the down loop with the morning Bala to Blaenau Ffestiniog train on 1 August 1956. The poster on the side wall of the station building advertises Newquay – a very different, and distant, part of the GWR empire from the scene pictured here. The roofs on the right-hand side show how closely the station was situated to the village centre, unlike those at Trawsfynydd and Maentwrog Road.

The platforms are still in position on 16 September 2006, some 46 years after the station closed to passengers.
H. B. Priestley, Pacer Archive collection/PDS

FESTINIOG: The rocky mass of Manod Mawr looms over Festiniog station as 7400 Class Pannier tank No 7428 arrives with an early afternoon train from Blaenau Ffestiniog to Bala on 29 March 1959. Just behind the coach is the signal box, which controlled the loop and sidings, while on the far left is the goods warehouse. The goods yard also contained a horse-landing, cattle pens and a two-track slate loading shed. The withdrawal of passenger services between Bala and Blaenau Ffestiniog was now less than a year away.

The track is still just about visible on 16 September 2006, while an informal path along the platform provides a useful short cut for local people. *Gavin Morrison/PDS*

MANOD: Three children pose for the photographer beside the attractive bay-fronted station building at Manod on 16 April 1958. Beyond the station the line curves around towards Festiniog, while the pointwork in the foreground gave access to two single-ended goods sidings. The ground frame cabin on the extreme right bears a cast-iron nameboard.

A covering of brambles partly conceals the disused track on 16 September 2006. A new housing estate occupies the land on the east side of the former station, the buildings and platform having long been swept away. *H. B. Priestley, Pacer Archive collection/PDS*

BLAENAU FFESTINIOG: After three years of gathering rust, the line from Blaenau Ffestiniog to Trawsfynydd was returned to use for nuclear flask traffic in April 1964. No run-round loop was provided at Trawsfynydd, and inward trains were propelled on the 5-mile re-opened stretch south of Blaenau. The 7T91 trip working from Llandudno Junction to Trawsfynydd draws to a halt for the trainman-operated level crossing at Cwmbowydd Road on 17 April 1985, with No 25058 providing the traction.

The same location is pictured on 16 September 2006, with rhododendrons and other shrubs spreading alongside and over the disused track. *Both PDS*

BLAENAU FFESTINIOG: 7400 Class Pannier tank No 7409 stands at the GWR single-platform terminus with the 7.15am train to Bala Junction on 15 May 1953. On the right is a short siding that could be used for loading and unloading vehicles. The hills overlooking the town have been reshaped by the huge volumes of slate waste produced since the early 19th century, creating the unique landscape for which Blaenau is famed.

BR opened the standard-gauge connection between the former LNWR and GWR lines in Blaenau in 1964, but it was not until 1982 that Conwy Valley passenger trains were extended to a new terminus roughly on the site of the former GWR station, also accommodating the newly extended Ffestiniog Railway. Single car No 153327 waits at the standard-gauge platform on 16 September 2006 after forming the 1314 service from Llandudno, while a Ffestiniog Railway Fairlie tank has just arrived from Porthmadog. *T. J. Edgington/PDS*

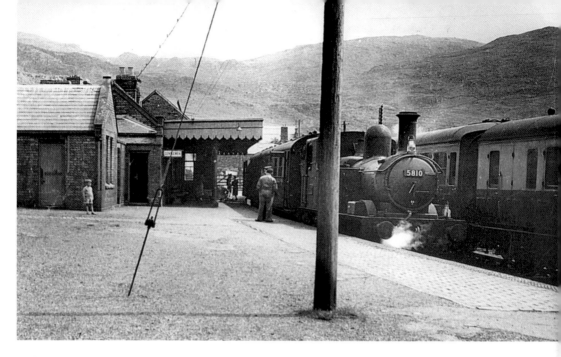

BLAENAU FFESTINIOG: A small boy sneaks a glimpse of 5800 Class 0-4-2T No 5810 waiting to uncouple from its carriages after arriving from Bala on 1 August 1959. Despite the rugged backdrop, the GWR station was situated right in the centre of the town.

The driver of single car No 153327 is poised to depart with the 1454 service to Llandudno on 16 September 2006, its 75 seats providing ample accommodation for today's meagre business. On the right is the run-round loop that BR provided to enable locomotive-hauled excursion trains to venture down the branch. On the Ffestiniog Railway platform a group of late-summer visitors waits to admire a Fairlie tank run round its train. *H. B. Priestley, Pacer Archive collection/PDS*